A Paines Plough and Soho Theatre production

T0049324

Sessions

by Ifeyinwa Frederick

Paines
Plough

Supported using public funding by
ARTS COUNCIL
ENGLAND

phf Paul Hamlyn
Foundation

Garfield Weston
FOUNDATION

ef Esmée
Fairbairn
FOUNDATION

Sessions

by Ifeyinwa Frederick

Cast

TUNDE   Joseph Black

Production Team

Direction   Philip J Morris
Design   Anna Reid
Sound & Composition   Asaf Zohar
Lighting   Simisola Majekodunmi
Movement   Yassmin V Foster
Assistant Director   David Gilbert
Dramatherapy   Wabriya King

Production Manager   Hannah Blamire
Company Stage Manager   Laura Haynes

IFEYINWA FREDERICK (Writer)

Ifeyinwa is a writer and entrepreneur. Writing alongside her full-time job as co-founder of Chuku's – the world's first Nigerian tapas restaurant, she has been featured in Forbes' list of 100 Women Founders in Europe. As a writer, her debut play THE HOES was shortlisted for the Tony Craze Award (2017) and Character 7 Award (2017) and longlisted for the Verity Bargate Award (2017). Ifeyinwa's new play SESSIONS will run at the Soho Theatre in 2021, followed by a regional tour. Fuelled by a childlike curiosity and fascination with people, her stories explore the intricacies of people and the dichotomy between how we really are and how society or we portray ourselves to be.

JOSEPH BLACK (Tunde)

After 10 productions with the National Youth Theatre, including LIVING THE DREAM for the 2010 World Expo in Shanghai as Oberon, Joseph graduated from Bristol Old Vic Theatre School in 2014. Since then, his theatre credits include: Clay In THE DUTCHMEN, Duke Orsino in TWELFTH NIGHT, Claudio in MUCH ADO ABOUT NOTHING (GB Theatre Company), William the Troll, Bombur and The Great Goblin King in the Duke Theatre's award winning park show, THE HOBBIT (UK Theatre Award – Best Show for Children and Young People, Northern Soul – Best Theatre Production), Stanley in A STREET CAR NAMED DESIRE (Rapture Theatre Company), Baloo / The Monkey King / Rann in THE JUNGLE BOOK (Greenwich Theatre), The Beast in BEAUTY AND THE BEAST (Salisbury Playhouse), Cleomenes in THE WINTER'S TALE (Cheek By Jowl), Lord Capulet, Friar Laurence and Prince in ROMEO AND JULIET (Orange Tree Theatre) and a European tour of OTHELLO as the titular character (TNT). He is also credited as the Fight Director of RABBITS by Sadie Smith, and ETERNITY by Asaro, and fight captain in most of the shows mentioned above.

PHILIP J MORRIS (Direction)

Philip is the Artistic Director of Trybe House Theatre following a period as Trainee Director at the Royal Court Theatre. His journey into directing began at the Birmingham Repertory Theatre (The REP) in 2015 where he started as an intern. He would then go on to become a Senior Youth Theatre Director. During his time at The REP, Philip was the instrumental lead in a pilot project named UP MY STREET which was created to work specifically with vulnerable young black men across the city. In 2018 Philip spent 2 years working as a Project Associate with the National Theatre with a project named NT Public Acts. After receiving training at the Introduction to Directing course (RTYDS) Philip has directed two showcases with Neighbourhood Theatre at the Young Vic in 2020 and 2021. He is currently working as a Project Associate at Company Three. A list of shows that Philip has directed more recently: 18 (Company Three, New Diorama), LIVING NEWSPAPER EDITION 7 (Heartband/Royal Court Theatre), LIVING NEWSPAPER 4 (Life's Work/Royal Court Theatre), NEIGHBOURHOOD VOICES MONOLOGUES (Young Vic), and SCENES FROM A BRUMMIE ILIAD (The REP).

ANNA REID (Design)

Anna is a set and costume designer based in London and a graduate of Wimbledon College of Art. Credits include: THE MEMORY OF WATER, CASH COW, PARADISE, THE HOES (Hampstead Theatre), DUST (New York Theatre Workshop and Soho Theatre), FOUR MINUTES TWELVE SECONDS, THE KITCHEN SINK, JUMPERS FOR GOALPOSTS (The Oldham Coliseum), LATE NIGHT STARING AT HIGH RES PIXELS, SCROUNGER, I'M GONNA PRAY FOR YOU SO HARD (Finborough Theatre), THE SWEET SCIENCE OF BRUISING (Wilton's Music Hall), OUR COUNTRY'S GOOD, A MIDSUMMER NIGHT'S DREAM (Tobacco Factory Theatres), TWELFTH NIGHT,

COLLECTIVE RAGE, DEAR BRUTUS, THE CARDINAL, SCHOOL (Southwark Playhouse), SOFT ANIMALS, FURY (Soho Theatre), MARY'S BABIES, DRY LAND (Jermyn Street Theatre), RASHEEDA SPEAKING (Trafalgar Studios), SCHISM (Park Theatre), GROTTY (The Bunker), TINY DYNAMITE (Old Red Lion), RATTLE SNAKE (Live Theatre Newcastle, York Theatre Royal, Soho Theatre), SEX WORKER'S OPERA (set only, National Tour and the Compagnietheater, Amsterdam), ARTHUR'S WORLD (The Bush Theatre), HIPPOLYTOS (Victoria and Albert Museum), HAMLET (The Riverside Studios). Anna was selected to represent the UK as an emerging designer at World Stage Design 2017 in Taipei.

ASAF ZOHAR (Sound & Composition)

Asaf is a composer for theatre, film and television. His previous work includes scoring, playing and performing in shows at Soho Theatre, Birmingham Repertory Theatre, Edinburgh Fringe, Deptford Albany, Ovalhouse and Half Moon Theatre. Asaf has been commissioned to score numerous productions for BBC, Channel 4, and Virgin Media, amongst others. Asaf studied classical composition at the Royal College of Music after years of professionally playing rock guitar. He has written scores in a multitude of genres and forms on commission, while specialising in contemporary production techniques.

SIMISOLA MAJEKODUNMI (Lighting)

Simisola graduated from RADA with a specialist degree in Lighting Design. Works in Theatre include: LUCID (New Public Company), TIGER UNDER THE SKIN (New Public Company), DRIVING MISS DAISY (York Theatre Royal), INVISIBLE HARMONY (Southbank Centre), SEEDS (tiata fahodzi/Leeds Playhouse), JUST ANOTHER DAY AND NIGHT (The Place Theatre), LIVING NEWSPAPER 6 (Royal Court Theatre), J'OUVERT (Harold Pinter Theatre),

PUCK'S SHADOW (Watford Palace Theatre), THE MASTER'S HOUSE (National Youth Theatre). As Associate: SHOE LADY (Royal Court Theatre), 15 HEROINES (Jermyn Street Theatre), HERDING CATS (Soho Theatre).

YASSMIN V FOSTER (Movement)

Yassmin is an artist, researcher and academic with a portfolio career in the creative and cultural industries. Her career is premised on a transdisciplinary work ethic, which is underpinned by her passion for movement. Her work as a movement director and choreographer is credited to: INSIDE BITCH (Clean Break/Royal Court), award-winning QUEENS OF SHEBA (Nouveau Riche), BOX CLEVER (Nabokov), WITH A LITTLE BIT OF LUCK and award-winning ALL WE EVER WANTED WAS EVERYTHING (Middle Child). Yassmin holds a BA (Hons) in Anthropology and Media, an MA Choreomundus – international master in dance knowledge, practice and heritage and is a doctoral research candidate. She is also a founding member of Legs Eleven Sound System: the nomenclature in the art of playing amplified music. This additional experience that informs her practice and allows her to explore aural, proprioceptive and visual perceptions within her work.

DAVID GILBERT (Assistant Director)

David is a director and theatre maker from Zimbabwe who has worked with the top leading theatres in London over the past 7 years. David has worked on projects and shows with Kiln Theatre, National Theatre, Young Vic, Unicorn, Almeida, Half Moon Theatre, Ovalhouse and Trafalgar Studios. He is a recipient of the 3 Month Regional Theatre Young Directors Scheme at Cambridge Junction, working on a range of productions by companies including UNIT, NEW INTERNATIONAL ENCOUNTER and DANCING BRICK. In 2018 & 2019, David directed shows at Brighton & Edinburgh Fringe Festivals.

In 2019, David took Young Vic's parallel production of THE CONVERT to Zimbabwe. Recently, working with Talawa Theatre as an assistant producer for their New Work department, David directed their 3rd short film as part of their series called TALES FROM THE FRONT LINE about profiling black key workers during the pandemic.

WABRIYA KING (Dramatherapy)

Wabriya graduated as an actress from The Oxford School of Drama in 2012 and qualified with an MA In Dramatherapy from the University of Roehampton in 2019. She believes that the arts have a responsibility to its performers to support their mental health wellbeing. This is clearly a shared belief as she is now the Associate Dramatherapist at Bush Theatre as well as supporting: ROMEO AND JULIET (Shakespeare's Globe), THE DEATH OF A BLACK MAN (Hampstead Theatre), SEVEN METHODS OF KILLING KYLIE JENNER (Royal Court Theatre), MAY QUEEN, BLACK LOVE (Paines Plough), SHUCK N JIVE (Soho Theatre), 846 LIVE (Theatre Royal Stratford East), TYPICAL (Soho Theatre), and THE HIGH TABLE (Bush Theatre).

HANNAH BLAMIRE (Production Manager)

Hannah is a Production Manager working on a wide range of projects including theatre, dance, circus and live events both in the UK and internationally. Her credits include SEA CHANGE and THE NICO PROJECT (Manchester International Festival), CAN FESTIVAL 2019-2021 (Chinese Arts Now), PETRICHOR (ThickSkin), WEST SIDE STORY (Royal Exchange Theatre), MUSHY: LYRICALLY SPEAKING and DISHOOM! (Rifco/Watford Palace Theatre), INSTITUTE, THE WEDDING and A LITTLE SPACE (Gecko), NORA INVITES: DEBORAH HAY (Nora/Saddlers Wells), HIGHTIDE FESTIVAL 2018 (HighTide), BROMANCE and KIN (Barely Methodical Troupe), ANDANTE (Igor & Moreno), HARROGATE (HighTide/Royal Court Theatre), DISCO PIGS (House Theatre), INFERNO, KENDAL CALLING, FREEDOM FESTIVAL, MANCHESTER DAY PARADE, THE MOMENT WHEN..., LOOPING THE LOOP and PRESTON PASSION (Walk the Plank), THE ROOF (Fuel) and IGNITION (National Theatre Scotland).

LAURA HAYNES (Company Stage Manager)

Laura has worked as a freelance Stage Manager for six years across theatre, dance, circus, festivals and events. Credits include Ockham's Razor, Punchdrunk, Boomtown Festival, Glastonbury Festival, Oily Cart, She Said Jump, Knuckle & Joint, Lady Vendredi, Paula Varjack & Co, The Yard Theatre, Upstart Theatre, Futures Theatre, BitterSuite and You Me Bum Bum Train. Laura also produces shows and tours all over the world with her interactive event companies Twisted Time Machine and Lycra 80s Party.

**Paines
Plough**

Paines Plough are a touring theatre company dedicated to new writing; we find, develop and empower writers across the country and share their explosive new stories with audiences all over the UK and beyond.

'The lifeblood of the UK's theatre ecosystem.' *Guardian*

Since 1974 Paines Plough has worked with over 300 outstanding British playwrights including James Graham, Sarah Kane, Dennis Kelly, Mike Bartlett, Sam Steiner, Elinor Cook, Vinay Patel, Zia Ahmed and Kae Tempest.

Our plays are nationally identified and locally heard. We tour to over 40 places a year and are committed to bringing work to communities who might not otherwise have the opportunity to experience much new writing or theatre. We reach over 30,000 people annually from Cornwall to the Orkney Islands, in village halls and in our own pop-up theatre Roundabout; a state of the art, in the round auditorium which travels the length and breadth of the country.

'That noble company Paines Plough, de facto national theatre of new writing.' *Daily Telegraph*

Furthering our reach beyond theatre walls our audio app COME TO WHERE I'M FROM hosts 180 original mini plays about home and our digital projects connect with audiences via WhatsApp, phone, email and even by post.

Wherever you are, you can experience a Paines Plough production.

'I think some theatre just saved my life.' @kate_clement on Twitter

Paines Plough Limited is a company limited by guarantee and a registered charity.
Registered Company no: 1165130
Registered Charity no: 267523

Paines Plough, 2nd Floor, 10 Leake Street, London SE1 7NN
+ 44 (0) 20 7240 4533

office@painesplough.com
www.painesplough.com

Follow @PainesPlough on Twitter
Follow @painesplough on Instagram
Like Paines Plough at facebook.com/PainesPloughHQ
Donate to Paines Plough at justgiving.com/PainesPlough

Paines Plough

Joint Artistic Directors and CEOs	Charlotte Bennett & Katie Posner
Executive Producer	Holly Gladwell
Producer	Matt Maltby
Technical Director	Colin Everitt
Finance Manager	Gemma Grand
General Manager	Faye Merralls
Associate Producer	Christabel Holmes
Interim Marketing Manager	Cherise Cross
Marketing Associate	Benjamin Willmott
New Work Associate	Phillippe Cato
Digital Producer	Nick Virk
Community Engagement Manager	Jasmyn Fisher-Ryner
The Big Room Playwright Fellow	Mufaro Makubika
Trainee Producer	Ellen Larson
Marketing Trainee	Molly Goetzee

Board of Directors

Ankur Bahl, Corey Campbell, Kim Grant (Chair), Asma Hussain, Tarek Iskander, Olivier Pierre-Noël, Cindy Polemis, Carolyn Saunders, Laura Wade.

Supported using public funding by
ARTS COUNCIL ENGLAND

SOHO THEATRE is London's most vibrant producer for new theatre, comedy and cabaret. We pursue creative excellence, harnessing an artistic spirit that is based in our new writing roots, the radical ethos of the fringe and the traditions of punk culture and queer performance. We champion voices that challenge from outside of the mainstream, and sometimes from within it too. We value entertainment, accessibility and enjoy a good show. We are a registered charity and social enterprise and our audiences are diverse in age, background and outlook.

We are mission driven and we measure our success in:

- the NEW WORK that we produce, present and facilitate

- the CREATIVE TALENT that we nurture with artists, in our participation work and with our own staff

- the DIVERSE AUDIENCES that we play to and engage

To create theatre we nurture new playwrights, we commission new work, we have our writing awards Verity Bargate Award and Tony Craze Award, our commissioning programme Soho Six where we collaborate with new writing companies on a year-long co-commission with an artist to culminate in a new play and, we produce new plays. SESSIONS by Ifeyinwa Frederick was developed through Soho Six in a co-commission with Paines Plough. Writers including debbie tucker green, Chris Chibnall, Theresa Ikoko and Vicky Jones had early work produced at Soho. With comedy and cabaret, we identify, develop and produce exciting new talents and present some of the biggest international stars.

We work beyond Soho taking work to and from the world's major festivals like the Edinburgh Festival Fringe. Our touring work plays across the UK and internationally with strong connections to India, Australia and the US. Our filmed comedy can be downloaded on our digital platform, seen on TV and viewed on international airlines. We're ambitious, entrepreneurial and collaborative and take pride in our strong relationships with commercial partners – but the profits we make go back into supporting our work.

sohotheatre.com | www.sohotheatreondemand.com | @sohotheatre

SESSIONS

Ifeyinwa Frederick

Acknowledgements

I first started writing *Sessions* on 11th September 2016. It started life as a nine-page short play – the longest thing I'd written at the time and the only thing I'd written other than my application to the 2016 Soho Theatre Writers' Lab. Writing was something I'd discovered that summer and I didn't know I had it in me to write a full-length play, speak less of having a career in writing. Since then, I've been fortunate enough to be surrounded by a beautiful team of people who have taught me, supported me and believed unwaveringly in me.

It is thanks to the collective energies of the people below that five years on from a very poorly formatted and clunky short play that the *Sessions* staged in 2021 exists.

The Soho Theatre Writers' Lab team for holding my hand through the playwriting process for the very first time and supporting me in developing my voice and writing my first play *The Hoes*. Holly Robinson for being the brilliant Writers' Lab buddy that she was and always saying yes to reading another draft. My agent Ikenna Obiekwe for making me realise I could have a writing career and for quelling any doubts I ever have with his pep talks. David Luff for introducing me to Ikenna. The Hampstead Theatre team for first putting on *The Hoes* and the whole creative team behind *The Hoes*, who made it the success that it was to propel me forwards. A special thanks to the cast, Aretha Ayeh, Marième Diouf and Nicola Maisie Taylor and director Lakesha Arie-Angelo, who pushed me as a writer in every notes session and whose lessons still play in my head as I write today.

Paines Plough and Soho Theatre for commissioning me, especially Christabel Holmes, Philippe Cato and Charlotte Bennett for their combined dramaturgical support, pastoral care and their commitment to creating the show in the right way for me. Daniel Bailey for supporting the play's development and introducing me to Philip Morris.

Philip Morris for being a director I could trust so whole-heartedly with the story, for putting his all into making the show the best it could be and for the constant laughter and good vibes throughout the process – a real g.

Joseph Black for working so conscientiously in and out of the rehearsal room to bring a loveable and vulnerable Tunde to life. The rest of the cast, David Webber, Kelechi Okafor, Gavin Joseph and Aretha Ayeh (again!) for each bringing a dimension to their characters that made the world of the play feel even more real. The full creative team who brought the best of themselves to make the show happen: Anna Reid, Simisola Majekodunmi, Asaf Zohar, Yassmin V Foster, David Gilbert, Laura Haynes and Hannah Blamire. Dramatherapist Wabriya King for creating a safe space for the team. Rebecca Need-Menear and Michael Windsor-Ungureanu for the captivating artwork. The team at Nick Hern Books for publishing the text and allowing the story to live on beyond its initial run.

The Black, African and Asian Therapy Network (baatn.org.uk) for helping me find the right therapist for me. Mimi Ogbe and Emeline Hanson for teaching me so much about therapy and myself, and for being the sort of therapists anyone seeking therapy should have the privilege of experiencing.

Sara Nisha Adams for being my person and a constant when things so often felt in flux. My mum and my dad for always respecting my writing and being unwavering in their support and encouragement – the best parents I could dream of. My siblings for being my rocks and their endless confidence in me. In particular, Chiamaka Aligbe for always gassing me, Adanma Frederick for reminding me to celebrate every win, and Emeka Frederick for giving me the space to pursue writing alongside growing our business. Abraham Adeyemi for reading the very first draft of *Sessions* I ever shared back in October 2016. Since then he has gone on to become a friend, a mentor and the greatest cheerleader of my writing. Everyone needs an Abe in their corner and I am fortunate to have him in mine.

And last but not least, me. For giving myself a chance at writing, for not giving up on *Sessions* and trusting myself enough to believe I could tell this story.

Ifeyinwa Frederick

Character

TUNDE, *an athletic-looking, thirty-year old British-Nigerian male.*

All characters in flashbacks are Tunde's impression of them. All other characters are to be sound recordings.

Note: Neither of Tunde's parents have a Nigerian accent. Tunde's Dad speaks matter-of-factly but is not intentionally harsh nor is he prone to raising his voice.

This text went to press before the end of rehearsals and so may differ slightly from the play as performed.

Setting

The play is primarily divided between the therapy centre where Tunde has been having cognitive behavioural therapy sessions and his bedroom in a studio flat. The onstage location should be set to Tunde's studio flat and the move to therapy sessions should be reflected in something other than a change of the physical space.

Tunde's flat is in the middle of being packed up with a couple of packed boxes and suitcases already together neatly in a corner. There are also a couple of bin liners of things to be thrown out. Tunde finishes packing up his room as the play progresses. It is indicated when music should be playing in specific scenes but there can be music in other scenes even when it is not included in the stage directions. When music plays Tunde vibes with it as he packs – sometimes subtly, sometimes more vigorously. Tunde's music is a mix of grime beats and hip-hop - think Bugzy Malone, J. Cole, Dizzee Rascal, Skepta, Lil Wayne, Wale. No music released in the last four years prior to the production should be used. Tunde's music plays from his phone so phone calls whether Tunde answers or not, cause a break in the music.

The therapy scenes are numbered to indicate which scenes come from the same session. Each session is a week apart. The bedroom scenes all take place on the same evening.

Additional Notes

The first # before a set of dialogue indicates a flashback to a time earlier than the current onstage action. The second # ends the flashback and brings us back to the time of the scene we have been following on stage.

In the therapy scenes // marks when we switch between Tunde's internal monologue and dialogue between him and Sandra.

[] indicates unheard (to the audience) speech from Sandra in conversation with Tunde.

In the bedroom scenes, *push* indicates a forward momentum for Tunde to finish his packing. He has a second wind, a renewal of energy. In the bedroom scenes, *pull* indicates a slowing down or a pause of the packing. He's hesitant, distracted, even hopeful.

Scene One

TUNDE's *studio flat. Today is* TUNDE's *birthday though there's no evidence of it in his space.* TUNDE *is sat on his bed in his coat and with his shoes on. He fidgets, indecisive, playing with a stress ball. Push. Pull. Push. Pull.*

TUNDE (*to audience*). If I get it in the box, I'll go. If I miss, I'll stay.

TUNDE *throws the ball he's playing with, aiming for one of the cardboard boxes. He really does try to get it in. He misses. Just. Push.*

TUNDE. Sorry Sandra, at home it is.

TUNDE *is deep in thought. He doesn't move. His post is pushed through his letterbox and the sudden sound brings him back into the room. He takes off his coat. He really is staying. His phone rings. He looks at the caller ID and he cuts it.*

TUNDE. It's Jag. Nah, I can't. He's been calling me for days. And Jag rarely calls unless it's important. He says this is important.

#

JAG. You can't turn 30 and we don't celebrate. Come on, T. I get not going away because you can't get the time off work. And I didn't even get offended when you categorically told me I wasn't allowed to organise a surprise party. Was I disappointed? Yes. But I was happy to respect your wishes because I thought you were going to suggest an alternative. But this is getting out of hand now. Now, you're saying we're not even going to go out out? I don't get it. Why not? Has Rochelle got something planned for you that you're not telling me about?

TUNDE. No, she hasn't.

JAG. Bro, are you alright?

TUNDE. Why are you asking stupid questions for?

JAG. Because T, you're the King of Birthdays.

TUNDE. And as king, I decree that this year I'm having a quiet one. Alright?

#

His phone rings again. He lets it ring out as he picks up his post. A particular letter catches his eye. It's a coloured envelope with a handwritten address. He opens it – a birthday card. He's caught off guard by the card, the message and the sender. He wasn't speaking but is lost for words. He's clearly thrown. He opens the card again to read the message.

TUNDE. Fuck... she...

Pull.

Scene Two – Therapy #1

TUNDE. She's struggling. Properly struggling. I haven't had this since school and I don't know how much longer I can listen to her butcher –

//

TUNDE. It's Adeyemi.

//

TUNDE. Apparently it sounds very exotic. They properly love that word.

//

TUNDE. Yeah, it's Nigerian.

//

TUNDE. She tells me the receptionist on the desk is from Kenya like it's relevant.

//

TUNDE. My first name? Also Nigerian.

[ ]

TUNDE. Oh. You can just call me Tunde.

//

TUNDE. They should really consider doing something to this room. It looks as sad as the people that must come here. It's just grey and empty. There's not even a clock on the wall. There's no clock. Fuck, how do I know how long it's been? I can't take out my phone. That's rude. But I wanna be able to know... she definitely just asked me a question.

//

TUNDE. Yeah, yeah it's my first time.

TUNDE *expects* SANDRA *to say something. She doesn't.*

//

TUNDE. Rah, she's smiling a lot. It's kinda making me want to hit her. Obviously I won't. But why is she smiling so much? It's like she's hoping if she keeps doing it maybe I'll start smiling too. Maybe that's what she wants. Maybe she wants me to smile so she can feel more at ease. Not gonna happen. Still smiling. And the staring. She's properly looking at me. It's fucking uncomfortable. It's like she's searching for something. I wanna tell her to stop but... I swear, the only time anyone tries to hold this much eye contact with me is when... maybe she fancies me. I wouldn't blame her. If I was her I'd fancy me too.

//

TUNDE. Sorry, I was... what is it I... You fix people.

Silence.

//

TUNDE. She's smiling. Again. Almost laughing in a polite way and tries to make a joke about not being a magic fairy. But I wasn't joking. If she's not going to fix me, why am I here?

She's using my name now and telling me how proud I should be to have made it here. I'm feeling a lot of things right now but, trust, pride is not one of them. I wonder if she'd still be saying the same thing if she knew I'd been about to leave when she called my –

What the fuck? Did I say that out loud by mistake? Because she's just brought it up.

//

TUNDE. I wasn't leaving earlier. Just wanted to get some water.

//

TUNDE. She points to the water jug between us to let me know there's plenty of water here. I hate her. Bitch.

//

TUNDE *smiles begrudgingly at* SANDRA.

TUNDE. Thanks.

[ ]

TUNDE. Well, I'm single and Hinge hasn't really worked out for me so I thought maybe I might meet someone in the waiting room. That said, I don't spot a wedding ring on your finger.

TUNDE *expects a laugh, a smile, a something.* SANDRA *doesn't respond.*

TUNDE. I'm sorry, I didn't… I was joking. It was a joke. Ethically speaking, that's probably not even allowed. And the other bit wasn't true. I mean I have been single a while but that's… I meant I've never used Hinge. Tinder I'm familiar with, I gave Bumble a go briefly but I've never used… Can you say something?

SANDRA *repeats the question.*

TUNDE. I haven't been able to get to the gym for a few weeks.

He expects SANDRA *to respond. She's waiting for him to elaborate.*

TUNDE. Okay... right... well... erm... you might not have
noticed but I've kinda got a certain aesthetic going on and it
requires maintenance. So normally I gym like four, five times
a week. But I haven't been now since...

TUNDE *calculates just how long it's been and realises it's
been more than just a few weeks.*

TUNDE. Well, the point is I haven't been. And I wanna be able
to go. So, I'm here. I guess.

[ ]

TUNDE. No, nothing's physically stopping me.

[ ]

TUNDE. I don't understand. I just told you. I haven't been able
to get to the gym.

[ ]

TUNDE. If that's not the reason, then why don't you tell me
why I'm here then?

//

TUNDE. I don't know if she's trying to be annoying on purpose
but I'm over this already.

//

TUNDE. Erm... was about three months before I got this
appointment.

[ ]

TUNDE. No, then I was going to the gym fine.

//

TUNDE. Fuck, how did she... nah, she's confusing things.
She's confusing me. She asked me why I came today not
why I... fuck.

//

TUNDE. Well, you weren't clear. I answered the question you
asked and you didn't ask me why I put myself on the waiting
list.

[ ]

TUNDE. I'm not avoiding the –

[ ]

TUNDE. No, I'm not uncomfortable. I'm fine.

[ ]

TUNDE. I said I'm fine. And if you want me to answer the question, I can answer the question. A friend had suggested it might be a good thing for me to try.

//

TUNDE. I don't know how else to describe her. It feels weird to call her my…

//

TUNDE. No. I don't know why they said it. I didn't ask. But I'm going to be thirty soon and self-improvement and that, so I put myself on the waiting list.

[ ]

TUNDE (*getting out a folded sheet of paper from his pocket*). Yeah, it's here.

TUNDE *hands the paper to* SANDRA. *He watches her read over it, uncomfortable. He tries to distract himself. The silence is too much for him.*

TUNDE. The options are really the same for every question, aren't they? I thought maybe they might switch it up halfway through. Test to see who's still reading all the choices properly. But nope. Every single one was the same. 'Not at all, several days, more than half the days, nearly every' –

Without looking at it, TUNDE *takes a booklet given to him by* SANDRA. *It's titled 'Coping With Depression.'*

TUNDE. Thanks.

He notices the booklet's title.

//

TUNDE. Why has she given me this? Why does she keep saying that… I'm not… And it's there again. She's saying it a lot now and I swear each time it's getting louder. I can't do this.

//

TUNDE *gets up suddenly and heads for the door.*

//

TUNDE. She's calling my name. I'm not looking at her but I can hear the concern in her voice.

He wavers at the door. His internal battle is visible.

TUNDE. What am I doing? We came here for a reason, Tunde.

//

TUNDE. Look, I'll sit down but just stop calling me that. I'm not depressed. I just need some help getting myself back in the gym. That's all.

[ ]

TUNDE (*sitting back down*). Thank you.

He pours himself water and takes a sip.

Silence.

TUNDE. She's breaking down the process, explaining what cognitive behavioural therapy means and how this will work.

//

TUNDE. So, we've got two months?

[ ]

TUNDE. You said we've got eight sessions. Eight sessions. Eight weeks. That's two months. And then what happens after that?

[ ]

TUNDE. Most?

[ ]

TUNDE. You said most people see an improvement in that time.

[ ]

TUNDE. But what if they don't?

[ ]

TUNDE. Okay, well, I need to be in that 'most people' category because it's my birthday soon and I wanna make sure I look buffer than buff. I can't be celebrating with one uncle belly. So you need to do whatever you need to do, to get me back in the gym so I can look banging on the day. That's the goal.

[ ]

TUNDE. 8th January.

[ ]

TUNDE. I dunno. I'd wanted to do something epic. And with as much birthday cake as possible. But... yeah.

[ ]

TUNDE. Ah, one hundred percent. Without a doubt it's my favourite thing about my birthday. But it can't just be any cake. There's levels to this.

[ ]

TUNDE. It's the same one I've been having since primary school. Victoria sponge with buttercream and jam inside. And it's got to have colourful icing. Blue, if possible. All the E numbers, I'm here for it. And it's gotta be properly sweet. I wanna be able to taste the sugar, you know. Like if you ate enough of it, you'd definitely need to see a dentist. That's the cake I have to have. I know, it's not very adult – my dad's embarrassed I haven't grown out of it yet – but I can't celebrate without it. Honestly, I love it.

//

TUNDE. She's smiling. I don't think she expected me to bang on about cake for so long. But I do properly love it. And normally, no matter how things have been, my birthday and my cake, it's something I still look forward to. Used to be anyway.

//

TUNDE. So yeah, my birthday, that's my goal.

[ ]

TUNDE. I thought goals were supposed to be time-specific but now you're making out like what I'm saying is unrealistic.

[ ]

TUNDE. But surely if we make the 'progress' you keep talking about, then things would be different by then.

[ ]

TUNDE (*quoting* SANDRA). 'Progress isn't linear.' I don't know exactly what you mean by that but it doesn't sound good.

//

TUNDE. I can't wake up on my birthday still feeling like this. I can't. What will have been the point of coming? Nah, she's wrong. I can get sorted by then. I can. Watch me.

Scene Three

TUNDE *is still packing. Dizzee Rascal's 'Sittin' Here' is playing and he is vibsing to the music as he packs. The beat is just about to drop when his phone rings, cutting the music.*

TUNDE. Who the?

He looks at the caller ID and cuts the call. The music resumes.

TUNDE. I wish there was a way that you could give people your number without them being able to call your phone. Or like it was socially acceptable to be like, yeah I'm only giving you this number so we can arrange sex. Don't ever call it. Ever. I'm not interested in hearing about your day like that.

His phone rings again.

TUNDE. The downside of being this good looking, they just won't leave you alone.

He picks up the phone.

TUNDE. Hey Sinead. Yeah, that's what I said. Siobhan. I said,
Siobhan... Yeah, that's fine. I was going to have to cancel
anyway. You just beat me to it. Yeah, it's fine. Next week? I
won't be around. I don't know when... Look, I've got to go.
Someone's at the door. Yeah, text me or whatever. Bye.

TUNDE *hangs up. There's nobody at the door. The music
resumes. Push.*

TUNDE. I just got cancelled on by Sinead. I just got cancelled
on by fucking Sinead. I've been stood up by a five out of
ten, seven if I've been drinking. Whatever, probably my
man up there protecting me from dead sex. She did look like
the kinda girl that would just lie there and let you do all the
work. As if being inside her vagina alone would be enough to
make me –

*A new track starts playing. Just hearing the intro has Tunde
gassed. He stops what he's doing. He turns it up and lets it
take over him.*

TUNDE. Are you dumb?

TUNDE (*vibsing to the music*). I remember banging this
nonstop the summer A levels finished.

TUNDE *is lost in the music, eighteen again. He's skanking
along and every now and then he adlibs and makes sounds of
enthusiasm.*

TUNDE. Ah man. That summer was mad. Mum and Dad had
gone to Naij with Kay. Money was a bit tight because we
were getting the loft done, so there hadn't been enough
money for a ticket for me too. Dad thought it'd be good for
me to stay anyway, to look after the house. Said it'd be good
training, would help me learn how to be a man. Dunno about
that. But it meant a free yard every day. And Jag and I made
the most of it. He basically lived at mine during that time,
and we lived on a diet of JD, bossman wings, and the finest
girls in North. It was... mmm.

*The sound of his phone ringing snaps him out of his
flashback.*

TUNDE. Hi Mum.

TUNDE'S MUM. Happy birthday son!

TUNDE. Thanks, Mum.

TUNDE'S MUM. Wow. I can't believe it. Tunde, you're really three-oh. You were so small not too long ago.

TUNDE. It was thirty years ago, Mum.

TUNDE'S MUM. It feels like yesterday to me. I remember the day you were born so clearly.

TUNDE. At least one of my parents does.

TUNDE'S MUM. Don't mind your dad. You know birthdays aren't really his thing. Now, tomorrow. Is Rochelle coming? I want to make sure I cook enough so she'll have food to carry home.

TUNDE. I told you not to make a fuss.

TUNDE'S MUM. So my firstborn, my son, my only son would turn thirty and I would sit there like a mumu and order McDonald's on the Deliveroo like English people do. Tunde, please, you're insulting me now.

TUNDE. I just don't want you going to any trouble.

TUNDE'S MUM. I'm your mum. It's my job. Now, Rochelle.

TUNDE. About Rochelle. Mum, Rochelle and I... we...

TUNDE'S MUM *squeals.*

TUNDE'S MUM. Oh, Tunde, I have waited for this day.

TUNDE. What?

TUNDE'S MUM. I was starting to wonder because I didn't want to be an old grandmother. I mean I would have preferred if you two had got married first but there's still time. Either way a child is a blessing.

TUNDE. Mum, you and Dad had me before you were married.

TUNDE'S MUM. Do as I say, not as I do, Tunde. So when is it due?

TUNDE. Mum, that's not it. I was just going to say that we... She's not coming tomorrow.

TUNDE'S MUM. Oh. (*A new thought occurring to her.*) Then I'll have you all to myself, then.

TUNDE *makes a non-committal sound.*

TUNDE'S MUM. You know, I'm looking forward to having you back in the house. Since Kay left it's been too quiet. You kids keep me young. You moving back home, it's... we're not supposed to live alone. It's not how we do.

TUNDE'S MUM'S *excitement makes* TUNDE *uncomfortable.*

TUNDE. Look, Mum, let me go so I can finish packing.

TUNDE'S MUM. Okay, okay. I'll see you tomorrow.

TUNDE *makes another non-committal sound.*

TUNDE'S MUM. I love you.

TUNDE. Me too.

Push. Pull. His phone rings again. He looks at the caller ID this time and he cuts it.

TUNDE (*to himself*). Jag.

TUNDE *resumes playing the track from before and through the music he tries to transport himself back to his younger days. He's trying to recapture that freedom but he's having to try too hard. He's vibsing to the music, but it's different now. He's more distracted. His mood has shifted.*

TUNDE. That summer was the same summer I started my list. It'd been Jag's idea.

#

JAG. You need a list. Everyone should have a list so they don't forget who they've slept with. It's common courtesy in a way and manners maketh man.

#

TUNDE. Jag's always been obsessed with courtesy which is ironic because until recently he's never actually been that good to women. Him at uni was the worst.

#

JAG. I know what you're gonna say. But she was basically stalking me. So I had to tell her straight. 'Babe, I'm not interested. Like I'm so not interested that if I tried to masturbate to the thought of your face it wouldn't work.'

#

TUNDE. And he used to have this theory... convinced himself that cheating was actually the right thing to do because that way everyone got a bit of him. Selflessness, he called it.

But he's been on the straight and narrow for the last few years. Treats Priya like a princess.

I never threw it away, so it's got to be here somewhere.

TUNDE *rifles through some of his belongings that he hasn't yet packed. No joy. He's about to give up when...*

TUNDE (*pulling out a folded piece of paper from in between a few notebooks*). Found it!

TUNDE *makes himself comfortable and scans the list.*

TUNDE. Rah, Jag was right because I'd definitely forgotten half of these names. (*Reading off the list.*) Tailah, Jess, Simone, Khalia, The Zante 7 – pretty proud of that. Audrey, Clarissa, Amma, Leah? Leah? Who was Leah? Skye, the one with the cats, Funmi, Jennifer with a y, Chisara, Precious, Baker Street, I remember Dionne – immaculate head game. The Tinder 10, Tara (or maybe Tessa), Kat, Rachel, Funmi 2, Amber, Eryn, The Cougar, Funmi 3, Rochelle.

The name catches him off guard. Push.

TUNDE *throws the list away and turns off the music. He notices the silence. It's a little too silent. But he continues packing with more focus and urgency. After some time his phone rings again. He was in the zone so it makes him jump. He's about to cut the call when he sees he's calling. Pull. He answers the phone with an energy we haven't seen him use before.*

TUNDE. Hi Dan... yeah, good thanks, you know me. What about you?... Yeah, I remember you said they'd come back to you before the end of the week. Go on, put me out of misery. Did I get it?... Cool, cool... Nah it's not your fault, market's tough... Next week? Mmm... I'm gonna pass. I... er... I'm going to pause the job hunt for a bit. Yeah, I'll call you. Okay, cool. Thanks for calling and er... have a good weekend.

TUNDE *sighs and lets the news sink in. Push.*

Scene Four – Therapy #2

TUNDE. She's surprised to see me again. I don't blame her after last time. But I'm here and I'm wearing my watch this time.

//

TUNDE. Well, I'd already booked the time off work so... plus I'm pretty sure the receptionist on the desk was checking me out last time so thought I'd make her day by showing up.

//

TUNDE. She wants to laugh but she stops herself at a smile. I wanna ask her if she's got favourite patients. I won't but I'm sure I'd be in the top five.

//

TUNDE. No, I didn't read the booklet. I already told you I'm not... Also, it was made using WordArt? You couldn't have really expected me to take it seriously.

//

TUNDE. She's stifling a laugh again. Not even top five, I bet I'm in the top three.

//

TUNDE. Yeah, about that, I didn't get round to doing the homework.

[ ]

TUNDE. It was a busy week.

[ ]

TUNDE. Yeah, I do want you to help me.

[ ]

TUNDE. I am trying.

//

TUNDE. Why is she lecturing me? I came back didn't I?
Doesn't that count for something?

//

TUNDE. Okay, I didn't fill out the sheet but I did think about
what you said, you know, identifying some of the difficulties,
I think that's the word you used... yeah, the difficulties that
I'm having. Anyway, I made a mental list and there's one
thing in particular that I wanted us to discuss today. Try and
problem solve, you know.

//

TUNDE. The look on her face. She's definitely trying to play
it cool but I know women. She's doing that 'I'm trying not
to show you you've made me smile but you've definitely
made me smile' face. Now, nobody can accuse me of being
uncooperative.

//

TUNDE. So, after last week I matched with this girl on Tinder.
Obviously, not Hinge because we already established I don't
use that.

//

TUNDE. She lets herself smile this time.

//

TUNDE. Anyway, so we match, we chat a bit. I mean, she
looked –

TUNDE *makes a sound, gesture, face or all three to indicate
just how good looking this girl was.*

TUNDE. But the good-looking ones can still be crazy or just
clingy, so there's got to be some vetting process y'know.

Anyway, she seems normal so she comes over on Wednesday
and we have sex and I... I... erm...

//

TUNDE. Ah I can't believe I'm actually about to say this. I
swear this shit better work and this needs to be the best
birthday I've ever had.

//

TUNDE. Well, it's more accurate to say we started having sex.
It didn't last very long because... erm –

[ ]

TUNDE. What? No! That... (*Pointing to his penis.*) He... we
don't have those sort of problems. No, erm... I started crying
during the sex.

[ ]

TUNDE. Not much more to say. I was inside her and I started
crying.

[ ]

TUNDE. If I knew why, I wouldn't be telling you about it,
would I? That's why I've brought it up. So, we can deal with
it. You said CBT can help me change my behaviours and
that's something I definitely want to change.

[ ]

TUNDE. Well, it's just not on is it... like, I'm sure my foreplay
was good and that but it can't really compensate for the nonstop tears while I was still inside her.

[ ]

TUNDE. Oh, she left pretty much straight away. I genuinely
don't think I've seen a girl get dressed that quickly but
she said she was only there to get drunk and dicked down
and hadn't signed up to deal with emotions. Which is fair,
I guess. I mean luckily in real life she wasn't all that in
comparison to her photos so I'm not too fussed about not

seeing her again. But y'know... it's not exactly what I wanna be remembered for.

[ ]

The question has clearly made TUNDE *uncomfortable. He doesn't answer.*

[ ]

TUNDE. Yeah, it has happened before.

[ ]

TUNDE. I haven't exactly kept count but of late it's been happening more times than it hasn't. But it's the first time a girl's noticed. Just another reason missionary's just not the one.

[ ]

TUNDE. Not much really. I wish she'd given me a blowjob first. I'm joking. She did that. Not that you needed to know that. I'm just going to move on. Any time you feel like asking me another question to make this less awkward...

[ ]

TUNDE. It made me feel... I dunno...

[ ]

TUNDE. Yeah, I definitely felt embarrassed. But it wasn't just that. It was like... like I felt disappointed?

[ ]

TUNDE. When it happened, once she noticed, it was like I could just picture my dad watching the whole thing. Not in a kinky way. I just... I could just imagine what he would say because he doesn't get the whole crying thing.

//

TUNDE. I remember the day I really learnt that. It was like the week before my twenty-first or something like that and I was just feeling... I dunno. I don't know how to explain it. I just had all these feelings and they kinda just came out in these uncontrollable tears. Like I was properly wailing – I'd never heard that from myself before. I must have been there for like fifteen minutes before my dad came in. I thought I was home alone.

#

TUNDE'S DAD. All this noise you're making, Tunde, it must stop. This crying, it's not something we Adeyemi men do. We are strong. So, please, stop it. You're disturbing my reading next door.

#

TUNDE. I kept going for like another half an hour afterwards. Into my pillow this time – to muffle the sounds so I didn't disturb his reading.

//

TUNDE. It doesn't matter. I don't live with him any more, so I don't have to deal with that.

//

TUNDE. It's like she didn't hear what I said or she heard and is just choosing to ignore me.

//

TUNDE. Look, I haven't come here to talk about my dad. He's irrelevant to the situation. I just want to be able to have sex without a waterfall coming down so can we just deal with that.

[ ]

TUNDE. He's been my dad for twnety-nine years. I've been sexually active for eleven of those years and this has only just started happening. So, annoying as he is, I'm pretty sure he's not the problem.

[ ]

TUNDE *looks unimpressed.*

TUNDE. Contrary to what you might think, he's not the centre of my world.

[ ]

TUNDE. Well, I don't know what else it might be. That's why
I've told you. So you can figure it out and help me fix it.

[ ]

TUNDE. No, nothing recently has... and before then... I guess
the summer was a bit... I've had better summers let's just say
that.

[ ]

TUNDE. I split up with my girlfriend.

[ ]

TUNDE. I can't remember when exactly. It's not like it was a
date I was trying to remember. But it would have been just
before I put myself on the waiting list. Rochelle, that was
her name, she'd been the one that had suggested I... you can
thank her for me sitting here.

[ ]

TUNDE. Five and a half years.

[ ]

TUNDE. No. She was the one who ended it.

[ ]

    TUNDE *shrugs.*

TUNDE. It is what it is.

Scene Five

TUNDE *is packing up still. His phone is on loudspeaker, he's in
the middle of a call.*

KAY. Happy birthday!

TUNDE. What do you want?

KAY. You're my brother and it's your birthday so I've called to
wish you a happy birthday.

TUNDE. No, you text. At best, a voice note. You're calling because you want something and you want it now.

KAY. Why've you got to be like that?

TUNDE. I know you.

KAY. Well, you're… can I borrow some money?

TUNDE. How much?

KAY. A hundred pounds. I'll pay you back, promise.

TUNDE. You still owe me five hundred pounds from three months ago. I won't hold my breath.

KAY. Is that a no?

TUNDE. I'll transfer you two fifty in a bit.

KAY. Two hundred and fifty? Are you serious?

TUNDE. You've caught me on a good day. Now get off my phone before I change my mind.

KAY. Thank you, thank you! You're the best. Love you!

TUNDE. You're welcome.

KAY. And I didn't just call about the money. I wanted to let you know your birthday cake is on its way to you.

TUNDE. What?

KAY. Y'know cake. Often eaten for birthdays and weddings. I know Rochelle will have got you one, but you can never have too much cake and I wanted you to know I'm not as selfish a sister as you think. Even if I haven't paid you back. Anyway, it should have arrived this morning but apparently someone in their office doesn't know the difference between 10 a.m. and 10 p.m., so it'll be coming tonight now. I guess you can have cake for dinner or take it to Mum and Dad's tomorrow. And yes it's Victoria sponge – got some god-awful blue icing on it with I don't know how many E numbers. But it's what you like so…

Silence. TUNDE *is touched.*

Tunde?

TUNDE. Yeah, I'm here.

KAY. Are you alright?

TUNDE. Yeah, I'm just…

KAY. Okay, well send me a pic of you and the cake when it comes. Bye.

The call cuts. Pull.

TUNDE. Classic Kay. She's irritating as fuck and makes being her older brother expensive as hell but you can never get fully annoyed with her because then she'll go and do something like that. I miss her sometimes. I'd wanted to go to Madrid to see her last month but… lent the bitch so much money I didn't have any left.

It's funny how our relationship's changed over the years. I can't lie, I used to hate her when we were younger. It wasn't really her fault, I just hated the responsibility that I got dumped with. Like all of a sudden, age four I became a surrogate parent. Anything she did wrong became my fault. Like when she got her first detention I wasn't allowed to go to football because I hadn't kept a close enough eye on her in school. Even now, apparently my year abroad ten years ago is to blame for Kay moving to Madrid. It's stupid.

I remember when she was four she had this thing about cows. She was obsessed with them. And she wanted to be one. She'd moo all over the house. That's the first memory I have of her being super annoying. And this one time, it was a few days before my birthday, I was going to be eight, and I was playing football by myself in the garden. Jag and I had this competition going on over who could do the most kick-ups so I was practising. And Kay comes out on all fours knowing exactly how to walk at this point and she's mooing again. Then she stops moving, stops mooing, ruffles the grass and starts trying to eat it. I was laughing at first but then I remembered all the worms that might be around and I tried to get her to stop. Mum came out as I was taking the grass out of her mouth.

I tried to explain but she didn't let me finish. She stood there telling me off holding Kay on her hip. Kay, giggling as if the whole thing was funny. And Mum just kept going on and on and all I remember was her threatening to cancel my birthday party and take my cake away.

But I hadn't even done anything and I couldn't say anything to make her... I couldn't say anything. She wouldn't have listened anyway. Would have got told off for backchatting then too and so I started crying. Like all the words I couldn't say formed into frustrated tears. Not gonna lie, I became hysterical. But it was my cake, man. You can't just threaten to cancel an eight-year-old's birthday like that.

Pause.

Then Dad came out. He didn't even ask what happened. Just told me off for all the noise and told me to stop crying. But obviously, when you're hysterical you can't just switch it off like that.

\#

TUNDE'S DAD. Tunde, it is enough!

\#

TUNDE. But I couldn't stop. I could barely breathe. All I could do was utter 'my cake'. So he took me inside, opened the cupboard, took my cake down from the top shelf and threw it in the bin.

\#

TUNDE'S DAD. Now you have something to cry about.

\#

Push. TUNDE *continues packing.*

TUNDE. Mum bought me a new cake for my actual day but I never enjoyed the party. I couldn't relax in case Kay misbehaved and it got taken away from me again.

The song changes. It's a Spanish-speaking artist. TUNDE *is clearly into it.*

TUNDE. This tune is a bop.

TUNDE *sings along under his breath, singing the wrong lyrics.*

TUNDE. I don't understand a word they're saying but it bangs. Kay brought me in on it. She had no money last Christmas – standard – so she made me a Spotify playlist of Spanish tunes she thought were me. She can be cute like that.

TUNDE *continues singing along, packing more slowly now, almost not at all. Pull. He makes a call.*

KAY. You alright?

TUNDE. Yeah, I just...

KAY. Hello?

TUNDE. Yeah, I'm here.

KAY. Why've you called, T? We literally just spoke and now you're not even saying anything and I'm kinda in the middle of an episode of *TOWIE* so...

TUNDE. I just wanted to say thank you. For the cake. I didn't say it before and I just wanted you to know I appreciate it. So, thanks.

KAY. You're welcome.

Silence.

Was that it?

TUNDE. You know I love you, right?

KAY. Have you been drinking?

TUNDE. What?

KAY. You never say it. I mean I say it all the time but you, you just say thanks and keep it moving.

TUNDE. That's not true.

KAY. It is.

TUNDE. Well, I just wanted to make sure you knew.

KAY. Well, of course you love me. I'm your little sister. And I'm great.

Shorter silence.

KAY. Okay, well I'm going to go now. And next time you
wanna be weird like that, WhatsApp me. It's less disruptive.
Love you.

The call cuts.

Scene Six – Therapy #3

TUNDE *checks his watch.*

TUNDE. Only fifteen minutes have gone. Fuck. I don't know
how much longer I can do today. I know she's talking
because her lips are moving but I can't hear the words. The
knot in my chest it's distracting me. When she asked how I
was, I didn't tell her. I didn't tell her I could barely get out
of bed this morning, that my chest hurts and I feel like I'm
suffocating. I don't know how to tell her what's happening
but I want her to notice. I want her to help make today better.

//

TUNDE. Sorry, what was the question?

[ ]

TUNDE. Yeah, I'm fine. Just tired. I went to bed late last night.

[ ]

TUNDE. Jag came round. We were celebrating. He's going to
be a dad.

[ ]

TUNDE. Yeah, he told me yesterday.

[ ]

TUNDE. Obviously, I'm happy for him. For him and Priya.

//

TUNDE. Only a dick wouldn't be. So I can't tell her that the
news made me feel funny and that's when the knot in my
chest started, because I don't wanna sound like a dick.

//

TUNDE. What else would I feel?

[ ]

TUNDE. No, I am happy for him, I'm just...

//

TUNDE. Fuck. I think I'm gonna... No. Not here. Not in front of her.

TUNDE *takes a couple of deep breaths.*

TUNDE, I'm good. I'm good. Did she notice?

//

TUNDE. It just caught me a little off guard that's all. I didn't know they were trying. And when he came over yesterday, I'd planned to talk to him... you know you'd suggested in our first session it might help my progress, if someone else knew I was... So, I was going to tell him... I hadn't figured out what I was going to say exactly. But I was going to tell him that I was coming here. But then he said what he said and... well, obviously I couldn't.

[ ]

TUNDE. Nah, it'd have ruined the mood. And I didn't wanna burden him with my shit when he was all excited.

[ ]

TUNDE. But it is a burden. I am a burden.

[ ]

TUNDE. Because it's true. Let's be honest, you're only here because it's your job. You wouldn't come back week after week to listen to me if it was just for shits and giggles?

[ ]

TUNDE *takes the worksheet pushed towards him by* SANDRA.

//

TUNDE. Great. Another worksheet. Apparently, what I've just said is an example of a cognitive distortion and she wants us

to examine it. I just want to lie down but I can't because I'm
here. And so is this stupid chest ache.

//

TUNDE (*reading from the sheet*). 'Evidence for this belief.' It's
what Rochelle thought towards the end.

[ ]

TUNDE. Well, no, she never said that. But, I mean, she was
the one that suggested I talk to someone. I think that's pretty
clear that she was tired of dealing with my shit.

[ ]

TUNDE. We had a conversation once about things.

[ ]

TUNDE. We'd been together about a year then and she'd found
me crying. I didn't really know how to explain it. So I just
told her sometimes it gets grey in my head and it's just
difficult for me to do things. I don't know if what I said ever
made sense to her but she dealt with it. And we managed
things together. So, when she told me she thought I should
'get help', it kinda threw me, if I'm honest. But it proves my
point.

[ ]

TUNDE. I didn't respond particularly well at the time, but
looking back at it now… It'd been three times that week that
she'd sat with me as I cried. So I don't blame her really. She
was tired. (*To himself*.) A weak man is no man at all.

[ ]

TUNDE. Just something my dad would say.

[ ]

TUNDE (*laughs*). Never. I doubt my dad's ever shed a tear in
his life.

[ ]

TUNDE. I'm serious. When my nan died, my guy was
completely fine. He looked more distressed when I got a

B in Maths GCSE. But maybe because he hadn't seen that coming. I was predicted an A star. Whereas Nan had been ill for a while, so I guess he had time to prepare.

//

TUNDE. She thinks I'm exaggerating but I'm not. I remember the funeral well. The sea of black gathering around this hole in the ground. I remember wondering what would happen if I fell in. Could you be both alive and dead? But I didn't need to worry to be honest. I was protected. Dad, Uncle Kenny and Uncle Sola were all standing there together, shoulder-to-shoulder like a brick wall, burying their mother, and their eyes so dry and ten-year-old me was crying enough for all three of them. I can still feel the sting from when Dad flicked my ear – his way of telling me to stop making such a racket.

//

TUNDE. He just believes that men should be men.

[ ]

TUNDE. I don't think he's wrong.

//

TUNDE. I'm just not as good at it as him. I'm not as strong.

//

TUNDE. What do I think he thinks about me?

//

TUNDE. That I'm a waste of space. A disappointment. His biggest failure.

//

TUNDE. I don't know. We don't spend much time together.

//

TUNDE. We've never really spent that much time together. Even before I moved out, having a conversation was rare. A lecture, yes. An interrogation, perhaps. But an actual conversation? Nah. And I remember this one time Jag invited me to play golf with him and his dad and they didn't stop talking the whole way there. Okay, so it was only like a thirty-minute drive but still. All I could think was rah, so you do this together every weekend. It was mad. And so, I tried to talk to him about it.

#

TUNDE'S DAD. What is it, Tunde?

TUNDE. I went to play golf this morning with Jag and his dad.

TUNDE *expects some reaction, acknowledgement or encouragement to continue. It doesn't come.*

TUNDE. Anyway, I thought it might be something we could do sometime.

TUNDE'S DAD. I don't play golf, Tunde.

TUNDE. Well, no, not necessarily golf. Just... I thought... Jag and his dad do this thing every week, and you and Kay have your movie nights. I thought maybe we could try doing more stuff together. Nothing special. Maybe a walk. Anything really. Would just be a chance to talk.

TUNDE'S DAD. What's happened?

TUNDE. Nothing's happened.

TUNDE'S DAD. So, what do you want us to talk about if nothing's happened.

TUNDE. I don't know. Just stuff. Life.

TUNDE'S DAD. I have already told you everything you need to know. Work hard, get a good job and don't get anyone pregnant unless you're ready to be a father. But when the right time does come, provide for your family. Everything else you will figure out.

TUNDE. But –

TUNDE'S DAD. You don't need to go on a walk with me to learn about life, Tunde. What you need is to become more independent and I'm not going to interfere with that. As your father, it's my job to make sure that you cannot only survive but that you are strong enough to support others too. So that's what I'm leaving you to do. Eventually, you will learn how to swim.

TUNDE. And if I don't?

TUNDE'S DAD. You will.

#

TUNDE. I didn't bring it up again.

//

TUNDE. We're just not close like that. (*Wanting to move on.*)
Should we finish the worksheet? (*Reading off the sheet.*)
'Evidence against'. Erm...

    TUNDE *tries to think of something. His phone rings.*
    TUNDE *looks to see who's calling.*

TUNDE (*picking up the phone*). Sorry, can I take this? I'm
expecting a...

    He answers the call.

TUNDE. Dan, hi. Yeah, now's a good time to speak I was just...
yeah, good thanks, can't complain. You know me. You?...
Great... Right okay... okay, er, well thanks for letting me
know... Yeah, yeah I'm fine. I wasn't sure about them
anyway after the interview so I think this just confirms we
weren't the right fit. Did they give any feedback?... Right.
Well, will take that on board for the next one. Sorry, Dan,
I've got to go, I've got another call coming in but thanks for
the update. Okay, cool, bye.

    TUNDE *hangs up.*

TUNDE. Shit.

[ ]

TUNDE. Yup. I'm fine. Can you just give me a minute?
(*To himself and under his breath.*) For fuck's sake. (*To*
SANDRA.) Sorry.

[ ]

TUNDE. Nothing. Nothing. It's just I really wanted that. I
needed that.

//

TUNDE. She's saying some stuff to try and make me feel better. And honestly, I just want her to stop talking and give me a hug. Which I know would be inappropriate and maybe if she did it I'd be weirded out because she's my therapist but I just want someone to hold me without me having to sleep with them first. I miss that.

Why is she asking me... oh yeah. I forgot she doesn't know.

//

TUNDE. I can't say there's anything wrong with my current job. I don't have one.

[ ]

TUNDE. I'm not working right now. Unemployed. Or as they say on LinkedIn 'I'm seeking new opportunities.'

[ ]

TUNDE. When I said last time I'd taken the time off work I was... call it a private joke.

[ ]

TUNDE. Hmm... about two months.

[ ]

TUNDE. Netflix has an extensive catalogue, so that helps.

[ ]

TUNDE. You're good with words aren't you? 'Left work involuntarily.' It almost doesn't sound as bad when you put it like that but, yeah, I was fired. Apparently, probation really does mean probation.

[ ]

TUNDE. Well, it means I'm broke as fuck. Rent still needs to be paid and I never noticed how expensive food shopping was until now. And neither Kay or my parents know – I haven't told them – so Kay hasn't stopped with her borrowing requests. And I'd promised my mum I'd help her with her flight to Nigeria this year.

[ ]

TUNDE. It's just not worth the hassle. They'll worry. Well, my mum will worry. Dad would just be Dad.

[ ]

TUNDE *is distracted and doesn't notice* SANDRA *speak. It takes him a moment to realise she's waiting for him.*

TUNDE. Sorry. I was... (*To himself in frustration.*) What is wrong with me? (*To* SANDRA.) Sorry, I... er... I really thought I was gonna get it. I hoped I was gonna get it.

//

TUNDE. I'd told myself that if I got the job then it was a sign that things were about to turn around for me. But I didn't get it and I'm getting the message loud and clear. Tunde, we're past help. This is pointless. Don't even know why I'm coming here.

//

TUNDE. Another exercise? We didn't even finish the last one. Not that it matters. It's not going to make a difference. Nothing will.

[ ]

TUNDE. You can call it black-and-white thinking. I call it seeing things for what they are.

[ ]

TUNDE. It is true. I'm turning up each week, I'm answering your questions, I'm trying. I even started the conversation this week. And yet, I'm not seeing any results. And to know that I'm trying and still failing...

//

TUNDE. I don't even say it because I don't want her to try and convince me otherwise. But what's the point of me being here? My life is a joke. What's the point of me actually trying every day, if I'm only going to wake up to more of the same shit. I'm tired. I want out.

//

TUNDE. Yeah, I know exactly how many sessions we've had. But three sessions is almost four, and four is halfway through, and I'm not seeing anything close to a fifty percent improvement.

//

TUNDE. She doesn't have anything to say back to that. Instead, she just asks particularly politely if I'll give the other exercise a go.

//

TUNDE *stares back at* SANDRA *in silence*.

//

TUNDE. It's the longest I've ever held eye contact with her. It's starting to make me feel uncomfortable but I'm not… She's pleading now. I mean she's not on her knees or anything but she's given me pleading eyes like 'It's Friday. I've had a long week. Please don't make this more difficult for me. Please.'

I want to tell her how much I hate this. How much I hate her. I want to tell her I'm done. But if there's even a chance she's right, that maybe I can be fixed, then…

//

TUNDE. Fine.

TUNDE *reads over the worksheet*.

TUNDE (*answering question one*). I am worried that I'll run out of rent money before I find a new job. (*Answering question two*.) Given I've been looking for two months now – and, well, I didn't exactly curb my spending in the first few weeks because I thought I'd just find something – then yeah, it's looking quite likely that this could happen. (*Reading out question three*.) 'How awful would it be if this'… is pretty shit on the scale? Well, I'd be without somewhere to live. My landlord isn't exactly the friendly, understanding type. (*Answering question four*.) I guess, if I did have to leave my flat I could move back to my mum and dad's.

//

TUNDE. Ah fuck. I swear the pain in my chest just got worse.

Scene Seven

TUNDE *is packing. There's a knock at the door. He pauses.*
He's not expecting anyone. He opens the door and is a bit taken
aback. There's nobody there but he picks up the cake box which
has been left on the doorstep. He shuts the door and puts the
box down and sits down, still a bit surprised, trying to work out
who it's from. He finds the delivery note.

TUNDE *(reading the note).* 'Happy birthday you miserable
cunt! Couldn't let this day go without marking it somehow.
Welcome to the dirty thirty club. May your hairline last
longer than mine did. Big love, Jag.'

[Alternative line depending on actor's hair: 'May this year's
blessings come as quickly as your hairline went. Big love,
Jag.']

TUNDE *laughs. He opens the box, and takes the cake out.*
It is just as he described to SANDRA *with a giant '30'*
on top. Pull. TUNDE *makes a call. He puts the phone on*
loudspeaker.

TUNDE. You sly one!

JAG. It's arrived then.

TUNDE. Dunno who you're talking to about miserable cunt but
thanks for the cake, man. Appreciate it.

JAG. It's nothing, man.

TUNDE. Nah, I appreciate it. I appreciate you.

JAG. Old age is making you soft.

TUNDE. Shut up.

JAG. Rochelle's been keeping you busy today, then?

TUNDE. What?

JAG. Well, I couldn't get hold of you so I –

TUNDE. Ah nah. I haven't seen her. I'm not seeing her... just
work's been a bit mad.

JAG. I thought you said you'd taken some time off.

TUNDE. Yeah, I had. But you know what's it like. I'm that guy in the office, so I just had to log on to do something earlier and it erm... yeah...

JAG. T, are you alright?

TUNDE. Yeah, I'm good, man.

JAG. You sure?

TUNDE. How could I not be? It's my birthday.

JAG. Which we're not celebrating.

TUNDE. I'm marking the day in my own way.

JAG. Well, I had something else for you too. But Priya said not to put it in with the cake.

TUNDE. So, it's not a car then?

JAG. On my salary? I'm not you, bro. Big money man.

TUNDE. Go on, what it is it?

JAG. Rah, why do I feel nervous all of a sudden?

TUNDE. If you're gonna ask me to marry you, I hate to tell you but bro, you're already married. Plus, you're not really my type.

JAG. Would you be godfather?

TUNDE *is silent.*

T, are you there? Did you hear me?

TUNDE. Yeah, I'm here, I just... You caught me off guard.

JAG. What do you say?

TUNDE. I can't believe you're asking me.

JAG. Who else could it be? I don't know anyone who I think could do a better job. I look up to you, man, and I know he or she will look up to you too.

TUNDE. Mate, I'm...

JAG. So, that's a yes, then. *Just tell Roch she needs to hold on for a few years before you two can have kids of your own. I kinda want my little one to have your undivided attention for a bit.*

TUNDE. Don't worry. You've got nothing to worry about.

JAG. Right, well, I better be going. I've got some stuff to do but, happy birthday again, bro.

TUNDE. Thanks, man.

JAG. And we will have that celebratory drink.

TUNDE. Yeah, yeah.

TUNDE hangs up. Pull. He wants to continue packing. He's distracted.

He goes over to his bed and lies down on the floor to pull something out from underneath it. It's a small storage box. He looks at it for a while and he has to re-psych himself up to continue. Still on the floor, he opens the box. It's clearly hard for him to see the contents looking back at him. He goes through the box pulling out various baby-related items – clothing, a small soft toy, a baby memory book. Going through the box, he relives the joy he felt at the times of his purchase. He sits there for a moment with everything laid out in front of him. Pull. Push. Pull. Push.

He packs the box back up and puts it inside a bigger box. He labels the bigger box 'For Jag'. He gets a text.

TUNDE (*reading the message out loud*). 'Happy birthday.' That's it. Not even an emoji. Thanks Dad, I guess.

Push.

Scene Eight – Therapy #4

TUNDE. She's smiling. And I don't feel like punching her, even if she does seem a little smug.

//

TUNDE. I can't lie, it felt good. Like I know, I'd have to get through two more stages before I get it, but just to get a second interview. It's like, okay... cool...

//

TUNDE. It's like, okay maybe she was right. I don't want to inflate her ego, so I'm not gonna tell her that. But it feels like things are on the up for me. Even today's session has been decent. I haven't thought about leaving once. So, yeah, maybe this was the improvement she was talking about. And this is what? Our fourth session. So with four more weeks... I think I'm gonna be alright.

//

TUNDE. I was even thinking when I get the job then I'm going to book Dubai for my birthday. Go for a cheeky long weekend with Jag. I haven't mentioned it to him yet because I know he'll get too gassed but if I tell him that's the plan, he'll be on it.

[ ]

TUNDE. Did I say 'when'? Oh, well. Positive thinking and that.

[ ]

TUNDE. But even if not Dubai, I'm going to do something. thirty's a big age, I've gotta celebrate.

//

TUNDE. And I'm starting to feel like I can now.

//

TUNDE. I dunno. Thirty just matters, innit. Like there's no doubt you're a proper adult then. Like twenty-five to twenty-nine is just training but thirty, it's real. If someone tells you they're having a child at twenty-five you're like 'oh, okay swear' but at thirty, it's normal. Marriage, children, a house – that's what you do then.

[ ]

TUNDE. Well, I'm not sure about that stuff for me. I think if your girl breaks up with you because she doesn't want to have kids with you then maybe you're not marriage material.

SANDRA *is about to speak.*

TUNDE. And no, before, you say anything, it's not me doing
that distorted thingymajig. It's actually what happened.

[ ]

TUNDE. I didn't think much about it until… but yeah I guess
I'd always just imagined me and Roch would have a family.

[ ]

TUNDE. Well, it didn't exactly make me feel great but I'll get
over it. I'm getting over it. Which reminds me. I had sex last
night. No tears.

//

TUNDE. I'll spare her the details but I'm pretty sure my
neighbours hate me now. But what can I say? When you
know how to please…

//

TUNDE. Does it matter?

//

TUNDE. My goodwill towards her earlier was a bit premature.
I'd almost forgotten how irritating she can be. Why can she
never let anything go?

//

TUNDE. I just don't see the point in talking about my feelings.
They're irrelevant. It's over.

[ ]

TUNDE. We were together for five and a half years, what do
you think?

[ ]

TUNDE. I don't know why you need to hear me…

[ ]

TUNDE. I just don't see the point in this.

[ ]

TUNDE. Okay, fine. I thought she was the one, okay? I thought she was perfect. For me anyway. But now we're not together, so I guess there'll be another one. And I'll get over it. I'm hardly the first person in the world to go through a break-up.

[ ]

TUNDE. I'm fine. Honestly, I don't think about it much any more.

[ ]

TUNDE. Yeah, at the time... I guess it was still raw then. But I didn't sign up for this because we split up. Bit dramatic going for therapy over a break-up.

[ ]

TUNDE. It was more because of what she said.

[ ]

TUNDE. I pretty much remember it word for word. (*Matter-of-factly.*) She said she never knew what was going on inside my head and she wasn't sure if I did either. And she'd tried to help with the 'moods' – that's what she called it. But she (*Quoting* ROCHELLE.) 'couldn't help me if I wasn't ready to help myself.' And for that she thought I needed to talk to someone. And until I would, the thought of adding a child into the mix... she didn't wanna do it. She said it wouldn't be fair. On them or on us. So, it was over.

[ ]

TUNDE. It was a bit shit to hear when she already had my child inside her but y'know. Life.

[ ]

TUNDE. Yeah, we'd found out a couple of months before.

[ ]

TUNDE. She had a termination in the end. Said she couldn't see how she could have the baby with me but she didn't want to do it without me.

//

TUNDE. I don't even know how she's done that. I just came here to talk about Dubai and birthday cake. And why does she look like she's about to cry? She definitely needs to work on her composure. Ah, she's doing the head tilt.

//

TUNDE. Well, that night I went out. I made Jag meet me after work and we went to some place in Shoreditch. It was a shithole but it did the job.

[ ]

TUNDE. He didn't say anything because he didn't know. I didn't tell him.

[ ]

TUNDE. No, I still haven't told him.

[ ]

TUNDE. I haven't told anyone.

[ ]

TUNDE. It's not anyone else's problem. It's not even my problem. It's just something that happened... I don't see why I'd talk about it.

//

TUNDE. What would I say? Oh yeah, so you know that girl I thought I was gonna marry? She'd rather have an abortion than stay and have a child with me. What does that say about me?

//

TUNDE. I don't know. I haven't thought about it. I guess they'll find out eventually but...

[ ]

TUNDE. What's that supposed to mean?

[ ]

TUNDE. I've got friends. You know I do.

[ ]

TUNDE. Well, that's not true I talk to Jag all the time.

[ ]

TUNDE. I dunno. Stuff.

[ ]

TUNDE. Okay, so I didn't tell him that.

[ ]

TUNDE. Okay, no he doesn't know about the job stuff either. But it just never comes up and I'm not going to bring it up.

[ ]

TUNDE. Because they're not things worth talking about. It's my shit to sort out and I'm dealing with them.

[ ]

TUNDE. I haven't got a problem being... I've been coming here for a month and talking to you, haven't I?

[ ]

TUNDE. You're going away?

[ ]

TUNDE. No. No, you didn't.

[ ]

TUNDE. I would have remembered this. You didn't say a thing. How long will you be gone for?

[ ]

TUNDE. You're going away for a month and you just forgot to mention it?

//

TUNDE. Ah, my chest is hurting. She feels bad, I can tell. She's saying a lot of words, trying to make me feel better. And now she's run out of things to say. She's just silent and blushing. It's actually kinda awkward. But she's fucked up and she knows it. It's not that I like coming here but I was just getting used to it.

Breathe, Tunde.

Why is this stressing me out? You're fine. We're fine. We've had a good week, remember? You're on the up. Maybe that's it. This is happening to show me I've got this. Exactly. I've got this. We have got this. It's just a month, thirty days. I'll be busy planning Dubai anyway.

//

TUNDE. It's fine. Just a bit unexpected.

[ ]

TUNDE. And just so I know when are you back?

[ ]

TUNDE. The eighth of January? That's my birthday. Cash gifts only, please.

[ ]

TUNDE. I swear, I'm fine.

//

TUNDE. She keeps giving me this look, like she's checking on me. It's like she doesn't believe I'm actually okay. But I am. I'm fine. I'm nowhere near as concerned about this break as she is.

//

TUNDE. You don't have to worry y'know.

[ ]

TUNDE. Because you are. I can see it in your face. I mean if you're that worried, you can always cancel your trip.

SANDRA *doesn't laugh*.

TUNDE. I was joking. It was a joke. Obviously, I don't actually expect you to… But I'm telling you, I'm good. I even went to the gym this week.

//

TUNDE. It's technically not a lie. I did go. I just didn't work out. I was in the changing room and all of a sudden I just couldn't. But the point is, I went. And that's progress, right?

//

TUNDE (*taking a piece of paper from* SANDRA). What's this?

[ ]

TUNDE. Right. Because you're worried that I'm gonna try and…

//

TUNDE. A 'safety plan'. She's fully overreacting. All because I didn't tell Jag one thing.

//

TUNDE *gestures his willingness to co-operate to* SANDRA. *He picks up the pen and starts filling out the form.*

//

TUNDE. I'm only doing this so she feels better.

//

TUNDE (*pushing* SANDRA *a piece of paper*). Here.

[ ]

TUNDE. Yeah, I know, there are only two names. I only put two people down.

[ ]

TUNDE. Well, you said 'crisis', right? They would be the only ones I would consider calling. I mean if I had to.

[ ]

TUNDE. Well, I think it's pretty self-evident why. Jag is Jag. He's my best mate. And my mum is my mum, innit.

[ ]

TUNDE. I'm pretty sure my dad wouldn't pick up. And I wouldn't talk to him even if he did.

[ ]

TUNDE. Nope, there's no one else.

//

TUNDE. Except Rochelle. She was actually the first name I wanted to write down but we haven't spoken since the day she went to the hospital for the… I figured it wasn't exactly appropriate. But this list is redundant anyway.

//

TUNDE. Yes, I've got it. If I feel... if things get... I should make a call. To someone. But I'd just like to point out that, I haven't thought about doing that for... it's been at least a week.

[ ]

TUNDE. Okay, fine... but what I'm saying is, when we first started and when I first did the questionnaire, I put down 'nearly every day'. But what did I put down today? 'Several days'. And there are only four options, right? 'Not at all, several days, more than half the days, nearly every day.' So that's pretty much as good as things can get. I mean there's 'not at all' but I think people that put that down are liars.

[ ]

TUNDE. Well, hold on... one minute you're telling me to pay attention to the progress I'm making. And now I'm actually doing it, you're not recognising that progress.

[ ]

TUNDE. You're not. You've just told to me take each day as it comes, like you're doubting me.

[ ]

TUNDE. Yeah, I've still got the booklet you gave me. Why?

[ ]

TUNDE. So why did you ask me to write the list if you were going to give me a number to call anyway.

[ ]

TUNDE (*repeating* SANDRA*'s words to himself*). 'Just in case.'

//

TUNDE. She needs to relax. I've got this.

//

TUNDE. Okay, I've heard you. And if somehow I'm wrong, I'll use the number. Now can we move on?

Scene Nine

TUNDE *tapes up the last box. The room is packed up bar a few items he would need the next day. There's nothing left for him to do but... he hesitates. He makes his bed again even though it's already made. He fiddles with a few things that really don't need his interference. He turns off the music. The silence is too much for him. It all feels a bit too final. He makes a call. It goes to voicemail. He laughs to himself. A tired laugh.*

TUNDE. I've never seen Jag without his phone and the one time I need him to pick up.

He's undecided about what to do next. He psychs himself up to try again. He calls his mum this time.

TUNDE. Mum, I... oh, Dad. Thanks for the text, it was... Is Mum there?... Oh, nah, it's fine. I was just calling to... I wanted to...

He's really struggling now. He sits down, places his phone down and tries to breathe. TUNDE'S DAD *can be heard calling* TUNDE *faintly through the phone. Still struggling, but trying,* TUNDE *puts his phone on loudspeaker and talks into it from where he's sat.*

TUNDE. Yeah, I'm still here, Dad. Sorry, the phone...

TUNDE'S DAD. Are you packed?

TUNDE. Yeah, I've been packing. I've just got –

TUNDE'S DAD. So, you're packing not packed. I have things to do tomorrow, Tunde, so you better be ready.

TUNDE. I'll be packed, Dad. Don't worry.

Silence.

TUNDE'S DAD. Tunde?

TUNDE. Yeah.

TUNDE'S DAD. Was there anything else?

TUNDE. Yeah, I...

Silence. TUNDE *sighs.*

TUNDE'S DAD. Tunde, what's going on?

TUNDE *is bracing himself to reply.*

TUNDE'S DAD. Have you got yourself into money trouble? Is that it? I can give you the money, just tell me how much.

TUNDE. No, it's fine, I don't need money.

TUNDE'S DAD. Then what has you acting like this?

TUNDE. I'm struggling to swim.

TUNDE'S DAD (*confused*). To swim? Tunde, I don't know what you're talking about.

TUNDE. You said I'd learn but I'm drowning.

TUNDE'S DAD. Okay, Tunde, I don't have time for your riddles. Please, use plain English. What is going on?

TUNDE. You never have time.

TUNDE'S DAD. Sorry?

Silence.

TUNDE'S DAD. Thirty is a bit young to be losing your memory but clearly age has affected you already. So, let me help remind you. The flat that you're in now, who helped you to move in? Every graduate job application – who looked at that for you? Who dropped you off at your first day at Warwick? In fact, who carted you round to all the university open days? But it's me that never has time for you. Me? The same me that has spent all of last week driving your mother around Ikea to prepare your room for when you're back.

TUNDE. That's not what I...

TUNDE'S DAD. Tunde, I have time for you. I have always had time for you. But you're thirty now. You shouldn't need me. You know at your age, your sister was on the way –

Push. The words hurt. This is not the first time he's heard this.

TUNDE'S DAD. We had a house and I worked two jobs to fulfil my responsibility to provide for my family. If I hadn't done my bit, then where would you be turning to now?

TUNDE. Thanks, Dad.

TUNDE'S DAD. I don't want your thanks. I want you to get yourself together. You only have you to look after – no family yet – and you're not even managing that. I'm sure I'm not the only one thinking it. Rochelle must have alarm bells going off in her head.

TUNDE. Well, we're not having kids anytime soon, Dad, so there's no need to worry.

TUNDE'S DAD. And just as well. Tunde, you're supposed to carry the load not be the burden. Just see how you're stressing out your mother. She should be resting, instead she's organising your room.

TUNDE. Yeah, well I told her she didn't have to.

TUNDE'S DAD. I don't want to be disappointed in you, Tunde, but… I'll see you tomorrow.

TUNDE'S DAD *hangs up.*

TUNDE. I don't think he knows how to feel anything else but disappointment towards me.

Push. But he's desperate for a pull.

He calls ROCHELLE *and puts the phone on loudspeaker, pacing the floor. It goes to voicemail. On hearing her voice,* TUNDE *thinks she's picked up and his disappointment is evident when he realises it's her voicemail.*

VOICEMAIL. Hi, you've reached the voicemail of Rochelle Henry. I can't –

TUNDE *cuts the call. He starts recording a voice note.*

TUNDE. Hey Roch. Long time no speak. I hope you don't mind… but your card… you said call if I… So, I called. I guess you're busy right now. But if you listen to this tonight and are able to call back I… I could really do with that. The right thing to do right now is probably to talk to someone but I don't have my therapist on speed dial like that – yeah, I started therapy, finally listened to you in the end. Anyway, you... well, you always said if things got bad. And they... it's dark Roch. In my head it's just this constant stream of bad thoughts. And I can't switch them off. And there's just this constant weight on my chest. It's suffocating me. Feels like I haven't been able to breathe for months. And I wanna breathe, I wanna be able to inhale and exhale. I want to feel alive not just existing. Like properly alive. The way being with you used to make me feel. Not like that, I wasn't talking about... Sorry I probably shouldn't have... I've fucked this up haven't I. Dunno why I'm telling you this anyway. We're not... this is stupid, I –

TUNDE *deletes the voice note and re-records it.*

TUNDE. Hey Roch, don't worry about calling back. Just rang to say thanks for the card. It was... It was nice. Thanks. Hope you're doing good.

TUNDE *sends the message.*

Silence.

TUNDE. Ah shit. I almost forgot.

TUNDE *goes to his bedside drawer and pulls out a box of condoms. He leaves the drawer open and as he talks he throws the condoms in one of the binliners of rubbish but makes sure not to put them on top and ties the bag back up after.*

TUNDE. I know they know I've had sex but I'd rather not leave them reminders. I don't need them imagining me doing doggy with some girl. Though maybe then they'd think I went happy. I mean there are probably worse ways to go. But imagine being the girl. Fucking grim.

TUNDE *goes back to close his bedside drawer. As he does, he spots something. He pulls it out. It's the 'Coping with Depression' booklet SANDRA gave him. He turns to the back where she said the number would be. Pull.*

TUNDE. It won't help. It might. You said you'd... fuck it. Fine.

He dials a number.

TUNDE. My name's Tunde… Adeyemi… A-D-E-Y-E-M-I…
my date of birth?… Sorry, is this the crisis line? Right, just
thought it'd be more… yep… okay… my date of birth it's
today actually. Eighth of January… 30… I'm calling because
I dunno. I guess it's what I told my therapist I'd do. I… yep
I'll hold.

TUNDE *tries to occupy himself in this time, getting
increasingly frustrated and fed up. He's on hold for too long.
Push. He hangs up.*

Scene Ten – Therapy #5

TUNDE *is ten minutes late for his session.* SANDRA *calls him.
The following voicemail plays out.*

SANDRA. Hi Tunde, it's Sandra calling from NEFLT. We were
due to resume sessions today – think maybe you forgot. We
have had problems with the text reminder service. If you
could give me a call back when you get this so that we can
reschedule. I hope you're okay. And happy birthday! I hope
you enjoyed your cake.

Scene Eleven

TUNDE *is lying on his bed in silence, thinking. He's playing
with the stress ball again.*

TUNDE. Bath should be ready soon. I'm not even a bath
person. Never really understood the hype. But my research,
and by research I mean my quick Google search, suggests it
might help. I thought about getting one of those bath bombs
from Lush – make it more appealing maybe – Rochelle
used to go on about how good they smelt but I thought
it's probably not appropriate. Regretting it a little bit now,
though. I mean how many corpses get to smell of vanilla?
Sure, the embalmer would have thanked me.

He goes towards the bathroom and stops for a moment.

TUNDE. I did think about writing a note you know, to explain. But I kinda didn't have the words. Plus, I didn't want to give Dad any more ammunition to be disappointed in me. So I thought packing up my stuff was the least I could do, y'know like to help.

TUNDE *heads towards the bathroom. He leaves his phone behind He's about to leave the bedroom when there's a knock at the door.*

JAG (*from outside the door*). Oi, birthday boy! Open up. It's frezing out here.

Pull. Push. His internal battle is visible, like in Scene Two.

JAG *knocks again.*

JAG (*to himself*). What's he doing? The food's gonna get cold. (*Shouting through the letterbox.*) Tunde, hurry up, man! Man's come to surprise you on your birthday and you're leaving him on your doorstep. (*To himself.*) I bet he's taking a shit. That'll be just my luck.

JAG *calls* TUNDE*'s phone. It starts vibrating.* TUNDE *doesn't know what to do. J. Cole's 'Farewell' starts playing.*

The End.

A Nick Hern Book

Sessions first published in Great Britain as a paperback original in 2021 by Nick Hern Books Limited, The Glasshouse, 49a Goldhawk Road, London W12 8QP, in association with Paines Plough and Soho Theatre

Sessions copyright © 2021 Ifeyinwa Frederick

Ifeyinwa Frederick has asserted her right to be identified as the author of this work

Cover photograph: Rebecca Nead-Menear; graphic design: Michael Windsor-Ungureanu

Designed and typeset by Nick Hern Books, London
Printed in Great Britain by Mimeo Ltd, Huntingdon, Cambridgeshire PE29 6XX

A CIP catalogue record for this book is available from the British Library

ISBN 978 1 83904 017 7

Woodland
CARBON
www.woodlandcarbon.co.uk
NICK HERN BOOKS
Printed on Carbon Captured paper